HANDBOOK

FOR
MANUFACTURED HOME
inspectors

Greg Madsen and Richard M. McGarry

Handbook for Manufactured Home Inspectors
Copyright © 2023 by McGarry and Madsen
All photos are by authors, licensed, or in public domain.

No part of this book may be used or reproduced in any form or by any means without expressed written permission from the authors, except for the use of brief quotations that may be used in book critiques or reviews.

The authors have made every effort to ensure the accuracy of the information within this book at the time of publication. The authors do not assume and hereby disclaim any liability to any party for any loss, damage, or disruption caused by errors or omissions, whether such errors or omissions result from accident, negligence, or any other cause.

Published by McGarry and Madsen
16822 SE 92nd Danna Ave, The Villages, FL 32162
mcgarryandmadsen@mac.com (352) 494-2437

Distributed to the trade by Ingram Content Group
ISBN: 978-0-9886651-5-6
Library of Congress Control Number: 2023909095

Table of Contents

Introduction 4
Site 7
Exterior Walls 10
Code Stairs 11
HUD Certification Label 14
Crawl Space 15
Foundation Piers and Tie Downs 18
    Piers 20
    Anchors and Tie-Down 23
    Vertical Ties 24
    Vertical and Frame Straps 24
    Longitudinal Bracing 26
    Lateral Arm Systems 27
    Roof Ties 28
    Tie-Down Upgrade Timeline 31
Belly Board and Vapor Barrier 34
Florida Overrides 36
Pit Set 38
Roofs 39
Additions 42
Performance Certificate 44
Wind Zones 48
Crowned Floors 50
Plumbing 53
Water Heaters 54
Emergency Egress and Smoke Alarms 57
Electrical 58
HVAC Systems 60
Termites 61
Park Models 62
Modulars 64
IBTS 65
Second Set Homes 66
Pre-Inspections for Moving 67
Tie-Down Certifications 69

Introduction

Manufactured homes are different from regular site-built homes. They are constructed in a factory on a steel chassis with wheels, towed to a homesite, set on a foundation that is often stacked concrete blocks on pads with tie-downs, and the wheels and tow-hitch removed. Their construction must comply with the HUD-code, America's only nationwide building code, administered by the U.S. Department of Housing and Urban Development.

The HUD-code is also unique in another way, because it is a primarily a performance-based code, while most other codes are "prescriptive." Prescriptive codes lay out minimum recipes for construction, with specifications for both material and installation. But a performance code allows a manufacturer to propose a new building product utilizing the latest technology and materials, and then have it approved by HUD, after meeting specified performance and safety standards.

Then again, manufactured homes are also the same or similar to site-built homes in many construction details, and must comply with local codes for connection of utilities, zoning, and setbacks. Also, any repairs, improvements, or additions after the initial set must meet the local code standards.

This book is primarily for home inspection and construction professionals with knowledge of construction techniques and inspection standards, who want to understand the difference between inspecting a site-built versus a manufactured home, along with the problems/defects that are common in manufactured homes. So basic construction/inspection standards, terms, and defects that are common to all homes are not covered. Although it would definitely be helpful for homebuyers, some parts of this book may be too technical for a layman.

Any time you want to refer directly to the codes, they are available free online.

HUD-Code for home construction:
https://www.ecfr.gov/current/title-24/subtitle-B/chapter-XX/part-3280

HUD-Code for home installation:
https://www.ecfr.gov/current/title-24/subtitle-B/chapter-XX/part-3285

Florida code for installation/construction, including "Florida Overrides":
https://www.flrules.org/gateway/organization.asp?id=42
and then select 15C-1 and 15C-2

The U.S. Congress mandated in 1976 that what were formerly called "mobile homes" must forever after be called "manufactured homes," in an attempt to rid the industry of a bad reputation for previous shoddy workmanship. But many people, and some state government agencies, still use the old name. We use both interchangeably throughout this book.

It is our hope that more inspectors become familiar with the details and idiosyncrasies of mobile home inspection. Twenty-two million Americans live in them. It is not a small market. Plus, you will be helping a low-income segment of the population that is vulnerable to quick-flip remodeler scams and can't afford to make a mistake.

- Greg Madsen and Richard M. McGarry

Site

HUD requires new mobile home installations to comply with their Model Manufactured Home Installation Standards, at 24 CFR 3285.203(d), which states that *"all drainage must be diverted away from the home and must slope one-half inch per foot away from the foundation for the first ten feet. Where property lines, walls, slopes, or other physical conditions prohibit this slope, the site must be provided with drains or swales or otherwise graded to drain water away from the structure."*

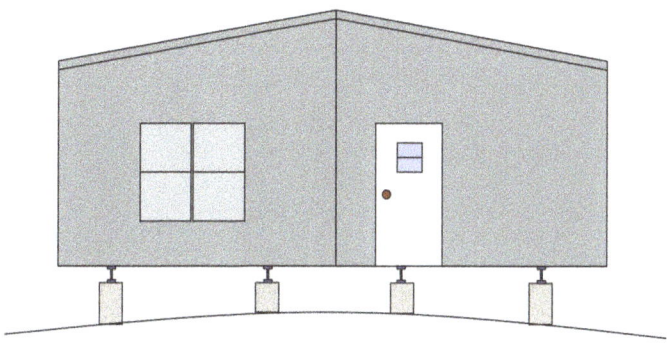

A shortened version of this HUD-code is "half-inch per foot slope for first ten foot away from home, unless other adequate drainage means is provided. Water must drain away from the home." This usually requires a raised soil pad under where the home is installed.

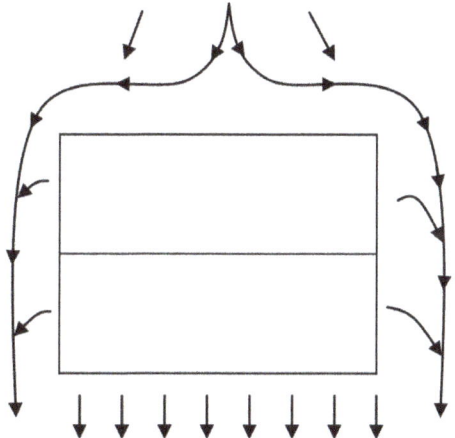

A home should not be installed on a flat site, unless swales and gutters are added to channel water away from the home.

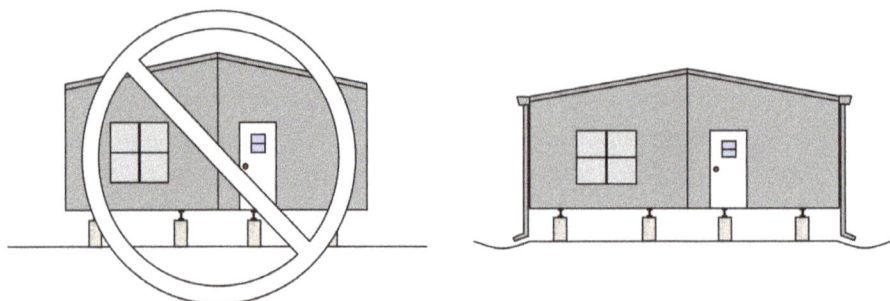

A home should not be installed on a sloped site without site preparation, requiring a pad under the home, along with swales and gutters to channel water away from the home.

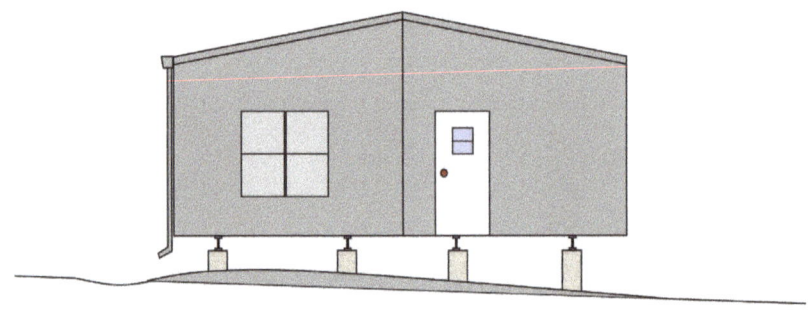

And last, home sites should be prepared so that there will be no depressions under the home in which surface water may accumulate. This is important. Small riverbed-like depressions running under a home, like in the photo at right, are an indication that proper site prep was not done and water is not being diverted around the foundation. Because most manufactured home foundations sit on top of the ground, any water flowing under the home will disturb the pads, cause piers to lean, and eventually lose contact with the chassis.

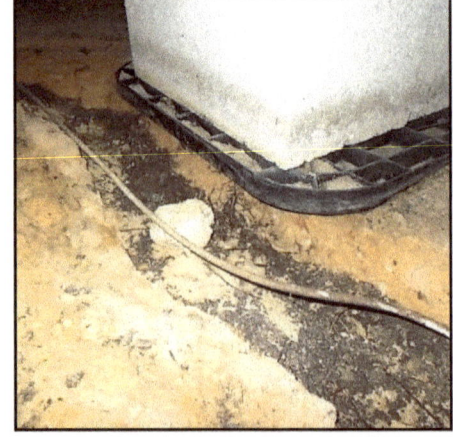

Unfortunately, many older manufactured homes were installed on a flat or sloping site, and do not meet HUD's site drainage standard. Soil movement over time or a homeowner adding soil for landscaping around the home can also ruin an otherwise good drainage pattern. And many homes have no gutter and downspout system to move roof water away from the home. It's always a good idea to recommend installing a gutter system for manufactured homes without one, along with rainwater leaders that deposit the water away from the foundation.

Site Checklist

1) Does ground slope away from home on all sides so that rainwater runs around the home?

2) If not, is there a trench and gutter system?

3) Are there any site-built additions that interfere with drainage?

4) Is there evidence that the soil and drainage pattern has shifted over time?

5) Is the lack of a gutter system causing a trough to form next to the skirting?

6) Are there any trees too close to the home, with roots causing foundation uplift, or may be a problem in the future.

Exterior Walls

Except for older homes with metal vertical siding you are most likely to be inspecting vinyl siding and trim. Depending on the era of the unit it may have composite, sheet goods or cementitious products. And of course the siding you are looking at may not be original. You have probably already developed a method for inspecting the exterior of a house, so use the checklist below in addition to your typical routine. ,

Exterior Walls Checklist

1) Is a deck or stair attached directly to siding, creating a water trap and bearing upon the frame of the mobile home, which is not allowed?

2) Does skirting sit outside of the wall plane (usually it's stacked masonry) that creates a debris and water trap and also funnels water into the crawl space?

3) Older homes with exterior water heater compartments are a great place to look for framing damage.

4) Many mobile homes have unroofed decks at the entry doors and, with the shortened eaves, door and window openings take on a lot more water. Check them carefully. An infrared scan may provide the only clue of leaks because of the vinyl covered interior wall panels.

5) Are there homeowner changes to the exterior walls with wall a/c units, stained glass, or lumber nailed through the siding, etc?

6) Site-built additions to mobile homes often show roof leaks and have siding below grade or ground cover.

Code Stairs

HUD requires stairs at each exit door from a mobile home, including sliding glass doors. Also, the stairs cannot bear on the manufactured home. They must be self-supporting.

But the minimum code requirements for the construction details of the stairs fall under the jurisdiction of the local building department.

According to how many steps down it requires to get to the bottom, the structure will be classified as either "stairs" or "steps." Stairs have four or more risers. Three or less risers qualify as steps, and have fewer safety requirements—but a mobile home is rarely that low to the ground.

Because there is less risk of falling, steps have no railing or handgrip requirements. Although a landing is not required at the top of steps by some codes, it is a recommended safety feature, especially where a door opens out over them.

Each local code is slightly different, but here are some of the generally accepted standards for manufactured/mobile home stairs, per the International Residential Code (IRC):

•• Minimum three feet wide. If door is wider, the landing must be at least the width of door.

•• Landing at top of stairs minimum three feet deep.

•• There should be a railing on both sides of the stairs that is a minimum of 34" high, with pickets not more than 4" apart—a spacing that does not allow a small child's head to get stuck between them.

•• Minimum 10-inch tread.

•• There must be a handgrip on at least one side of the stairs. The handgrip must be small enough to easily wrap your hand around. If it is separate from the railing, then the ends must return back to the railing cap, wall, or end post so that it is not possible to snag a handbag or sleeve on the end and tumble down. Handgrips must be between 34" and 38" above the nosing of the treads.

•• Risers should not exceed seven and three-quarters inches high, with not more than a quarter inch variation in height between risers. The first and last risers are where we typically see any change in riser height.

Here's an example of the typical requirements, from the City of Coeur d'Alene, Idaho.

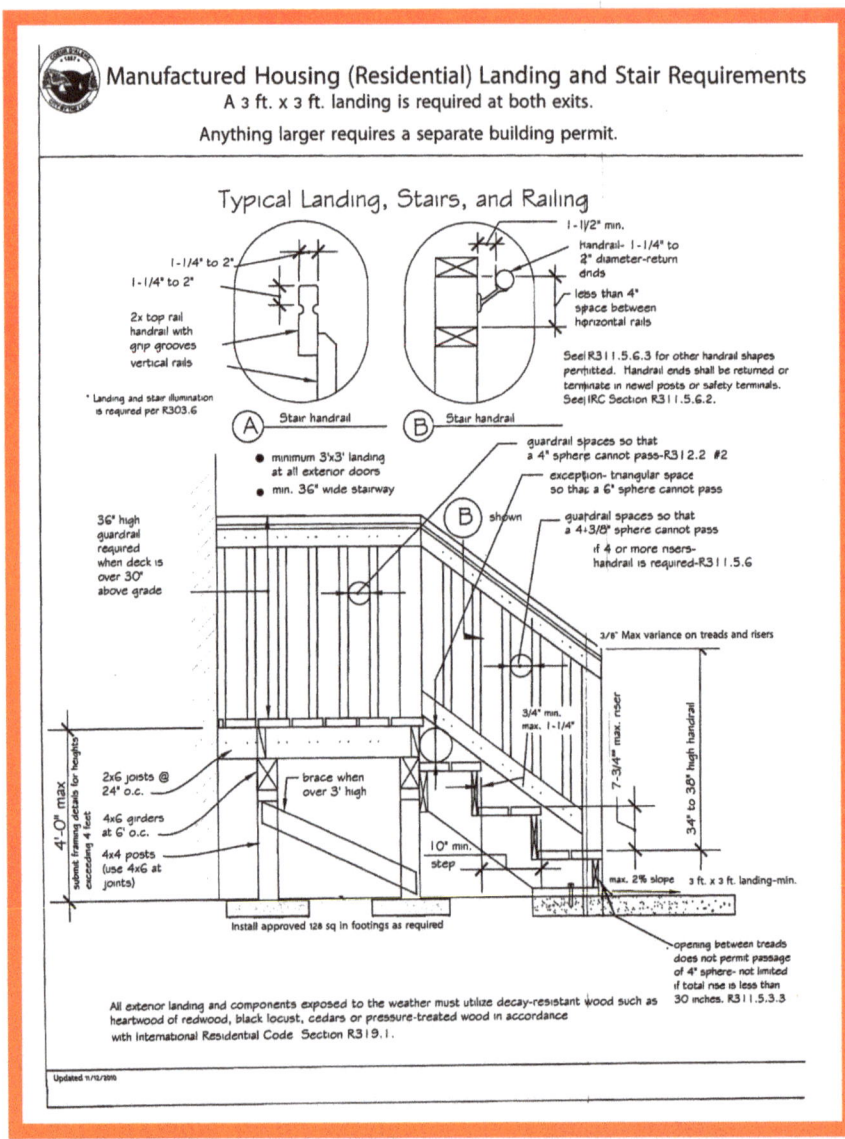

Code Stairs Checklist

1) Does a sliding glass door have both sections moveable, but stairs across only one side? Either one door panel should be permanently fixed in place, or the stairs should span the entire width of the door.

2) Is there lack of a landing at top of stair?

3) Are there uneven risers, especially first or last one?

4) Is there more than 4" between railing pickets?

5) Is there a handrail that you can easily wrap your hand around to securely grab it, maximum 2" diameter.

6) Are there missing code stairs at an exit door. Because a manufactured home is required to have two functional egress doors, disabling the second door is not an option.

HUD Certification Label

The HUD Certification Label is a 2 inch by 4 inch red metal plate riveted to the exterior wall of each section of mobile home. Some folks call it a "HUD Label," others say "red tag," but the official name used by HUD is Certification Label. The tag has a stamped serial number that identifies that particular home, or section of a home, in HUD records. You will only find it on homes manufactured under HUD jurisdiction after July 15, 1976.

Although a HUD tag starts off life bright red, the color gradually fades to pale red, and older tags sometimes have no color at all. Because the number is stamped into the metal, the loss of color does not affect readability of the tag.

The tag can be found near the bottom of one of the ends of a single-wide home, close to a corner. It is often on the long side of each unit of a multi-wide home and low, near the corner, because the siding on the short side is typically installed at the site after joining the sections.

We recommend that you locate and document the HUD tag number as part of an inspection, and note if any HUD tags are missing. If the HUD Performance Certificate inside the home is missing—which is often the case in older homes—then the HUD tag number provides a way for the homebuyer to get the complete data on the manufacture of the home from IBTS (see page 65).

Crawl Space

Where is the best place to enter the crawl space? It all depends on how the house is sited, what additions have been made and what type of skirting is installed. If the skirting material is solid you may only have one choice.

The HUD minimum size requirement for a manufactured-mobile home access panel is 18-inches wide by 24-inches high and not less than 3 square feet in total area [24CFR3285.505(e)]. The access panel(s) must be located so that any water supply or sewer drain connections are accessible. Because installation details are also under the jurisdiction of the local building department, you should check for any additional requirements they may have. An example of a typical local code requirement would be that the access panel must be openable without any special tools.

Most homes have the type of skirting shown below, which has a U-shaped track at the bottom and a flap covering the top of the interlocking skirt panels. Removing two adjacent panels is sufficient for access. You can usually flip up the top flap enough to pull two panels up without having to snap it out of its securing strip. But, if not, it's easy enough to pull out a section of flap, then snap it back in place when you are done.

The panels are typically secured with screws at the top. They often have a hex-head, so you may need a hex driver. Also, dirt may get into the bottom track as you crawl over it and will have to be removed when you are done, in order to get the skirt panels to slide all the way back down into the track.

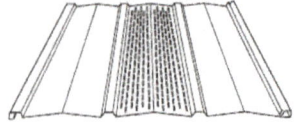 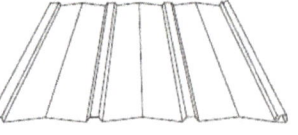 

Skirting with ventilation   Skirting without ventilation   Typical vent

Other types of skirting, such as brick or stucco over wire lath, will mean you can only get under the home at an installed access panel. Many times this limits your ability to get a good look at the entire crawl space because of obstructions.

Under a window leak

Over the years you may build your own collection of wacky skirting materials photos. We have seen everything from shipping pallets to lines of wood stakes. Sometimes the best that you can do is to try to find a few places to stick your hand in and snap a bunch of pictures.

Time Saver

This tool makes it easier to reattach the siding by running it along the groove as you press the pieces together. But wait! Before you decide against putting another gadget in your toolbox, there's more: the zipper also makes it easier to detach and reconnect the rail strip along the top of mobile home skirting when accessing a crawl space. Expect to pay about $10.

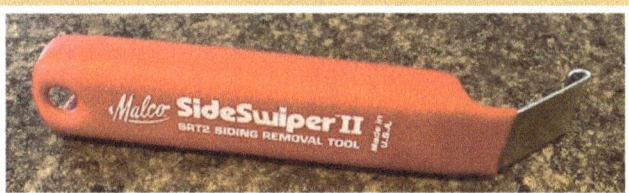

And you can pay a little more at $15 for our personal favorite: a combination vinyl zipper, mini pry bar, and nail puller. Both are available at Amazon and most big-box home improvement stores.

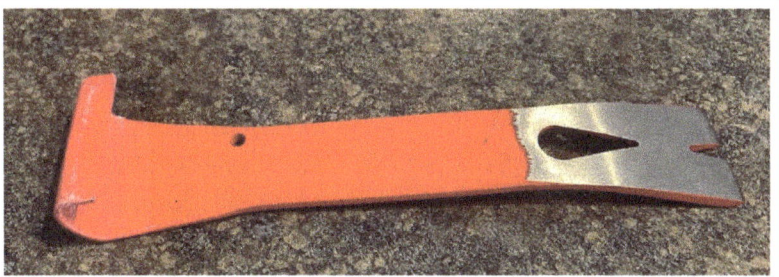

Foundation Piers and Tie Downs

Inspecting a mobile home crawlspace can be tricky when there is limited access and, unfortunately, that happens fairly often. So a little planning at the beginning of an inspection can save a lot crawling. Walking once around the perimeter of the home will let you know where the obstacles to access are located: bathroom and kitchen windows indicate plumbing below, and the area behind the package a/c unit has the main supply and return ducts that divide the crawlspace into sections. If the home has removable skirting, entering at a couple of locations may be the only way to view most of a crawlspace.

Sighting down the sides of the home for bows or dips in the skirting and trim can help locate where to look in the crawlspace for potential problems. Gutter downspouts or lack of gutters can move soil over time effecting the piers directly behind the skirting. Trees close to the home can disrupt piers with root growth and changes in soil moisture content. How well the site was prepared for the home will determine the stability of the piers over time.

The permanent foundation components are typically piers of stacked block on concrete or plastic pads with wood shims below the frame and anchor rods in the soil with straps attaching to the steel frame. Longitudinal bracing is also now required.

The U.S. Department of Housing and Urban Development (HUD) includes this definition of a permanent foundation in their publication Permanent Foundations Guide for Manufactured Housing:

C. Definition of Permanent Foundation

Permanent foundations must be constructed of durable materials; i.e. concrete, mortared masonry, or treated wood - and be site-built. It shall have attachment points to anchor and stabilize the manufactured home to transfer all loads, herein defined, to the underlying soil or rock. The permanent foundations shall be structurally developed in accordance with this document or be structurally designed by a licensed professional engineer for the following::

1. Vertical stability:

a. Rated anchorage capacity to prevent uplift and overturning due to wind or seismic forces, whichever controls. Screw-in soil anchors at not considered a permanent anchorage.

b. Footing size to prevent overloading the soil-bearing capacity and avoids soil settlement. Footing shall be reinforced concrete to be considered permanent.

c. Base of footing below maximum frost-penetration depth.

d. Enclosed basement of crawl space with a continuous wall (whether bear or non-bearing) that separates the basement crawl space from the backfill, and keeps out vermin and water.

2. Lateral stability. Rated anchorage capacity to prevent sliding due to wind or seismic forces, whichever controls, in the transverse and longitudinal direction.

Here's the key facts to note in the HUD definition of a permanent foundation:

1) A permanent foundation system can either follow the standards of the HUD guide OR be designed by a licensed professional engineer.

2) Although it states that the screw-in anchors that are commonly used "are not considered a permanent foundation system," they can be used in conjunction with a longitudinal stabilization bracing system, and the combination can be certified by a professional engineer as a permanent foundation.

3) The maximum frost penetration depth is an issue in other states, but in Florida it's zero inches.

4) A permanent foundation is necessary to get FHA financing for a mobile home.

A different definition of a permanent foundation may be used by local tax officials in the jurisdiction where home will be sited. If the home has had the tow bar, axles, and tires removed, and is secured on a standard "stacked block on pads, with screw-in soil anchors and longitudinal bracing" foundation, then it fits the definition in most areas as a permanent foundation for taxation as real estate instead of personal property–as long as both the home and land are owned (not in a park).

Piers

Pads should be a minimum 16"x16" and 4" thick precast concrete pad on grade, although you may have to dig to confirm this if there has been soil movement in the crawlspace. An alternative is a plastic pier pad that is specified by the manufacturer for loads and soil bearing and will always extend several inches past the pier footprint as it aligns with the shape of the block. Any other materials are not rated. Homeowner installed floor supports of 4x4s, landscape timbers, etc. indicate a pier or flooring defect in the vicinity.

The pier column is of vertically oriented open cell 8"x8"x16" concrete block. Piers are used in a single column or double stacked interlocked configuration. The piers should be centered under the I-beam and the wood shims will be 3-1/2" x 6" with a height of 1" for a new home and up to 1-1/2" for a used home. A pier that is over shimmed tells a the tale of a quick fix to a settlement problem. Required at the top of the block column is a precast concrete cap block or pressure treated lumber that is 2"x8"x16". Cracked cap blocks or multiple layers of lumber are not approved.

There are two HUD specs for block piers, one for piers up to 36" high using single-stacked blocks, and another for piers from 36" to 67" with double-stacked blocks, per HUD CFR 3285.306, and as shown below. The Florida Override specifies a higher standard for corner piers over 24-inches: they must be double tiered with interlocking blocks.

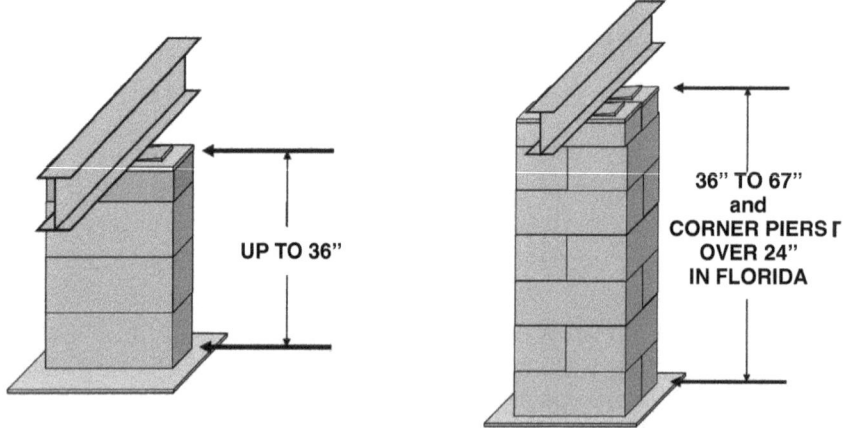

Piers over 67" high must be designed by a licensed engineer or architect. Mortar is not required unless specified by the manufacturer and, since these are minimum requirements, the manufacturer's specifications may exceed them.

The minimum height allowed in Florida between the ground under all new and used mobile homes and the bottom of the I-beam is 18-inches. When the grade is sloped, 25% of the lowest part of the main frame is allowed below 18-inches. But no part of the bottom of the I-beam can be below 12-inches from the ground. HUD is more lenient and allows a minimum clearance of 12-inches between ground and bottom of beam in other states.

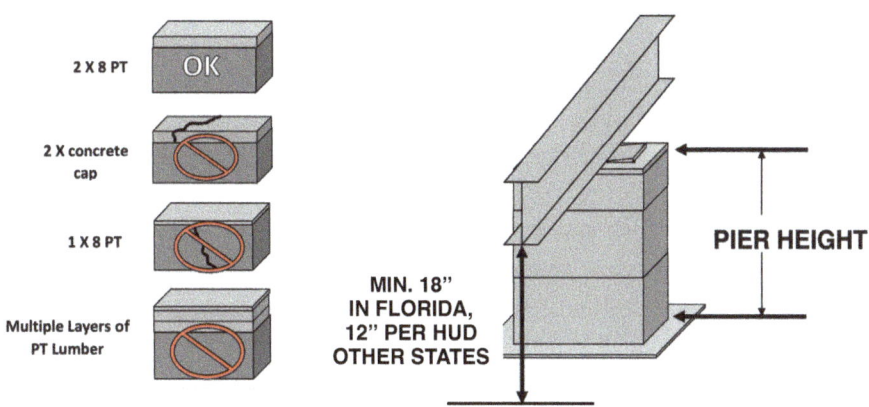

Sighting down the rows of piers will reveal any leaning piers or lack of contact with the frame. Center line piers typically have spaces between them at the large wall openings, however any center line opening of more than 10' requires blocking. If you find a river bed in the crawlspace, follow it to find the pier defects that it has caused.

Here is a list of some common defects you may encounter:
1) Concrete blocks sit on pad in wrong direction.
2) Block piers not centered on pad.
3) Piers not perpendicular to the I beam.
4) Piers not perpendicular to the centerline.
5) Piers have settled, have loose shims or too many shims.
6) Cracked or chipped block.
7) Cap blocks incorrect size and/or material.

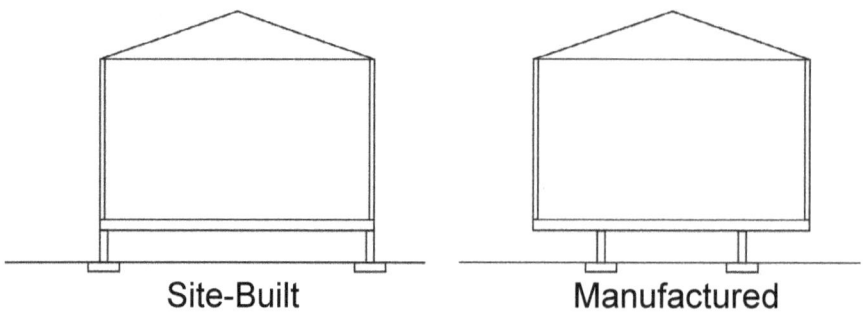

Site-Built   Manufactured

A big difference between manufactured and site-built homes is that the stem walls for site-built are located under the exterior walls and mobile home piers are aligned below the metal frame inward from the wall edge.

Pier design and placement is specific to the individual unit. Many factors from soil load bearing to manufacturer's specifications determine the configuration and placement of the piers. This is information that an inspector cannot verify, so a clear understanding of the floor plan will be helpful when in the crawlspace. The large openings in the centerline of the home, exterior door openings, fireplaces and bay windows require piers designed to accomodate the additional transfer of loads.

Here is a checklist of easy to identify defects:
1) The first piers should be within 2-feet of either end of the home.
2) Center line piers should be within 2-feet of either end of the home and spaced at no more than 8-feet on center except where openings of 4-feet or more occur.
3) Any openings more than 15-feet in the exterior side wall or marriage wall requires blocking at each end of the opening with three 4"x16"x16" stacked concrete pads or equivalent for increased soil bearing.

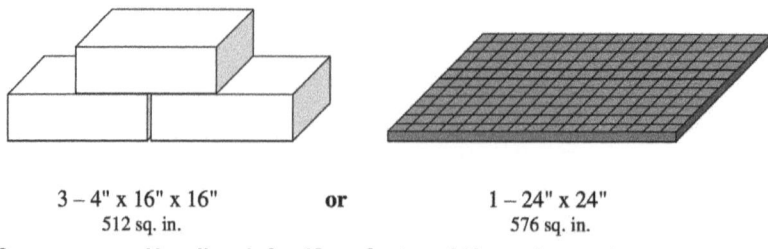

3 – 4" x 16" x 16"   or   1 – 24" x 24"
512 sq. in.   576 sq. in.

Anchors and Tie-Downs

Augered anchor rods have a helical tip and are most efficient in the sandy Florida soil. Other soil situations call for different types of anchors - hard rock anchors, drive anchors, concrete deadmen or anchors in a concrete slab. Only the head of the augered anchor, set flush with the grade, and the stabilizer plate pressed against it parallel to the sidewall above should be visible. All components should be corrosion free.

All anchors are required to be installed in the vertical position. You may see sidewall anchors and thier straps at a slight angle to accomodate the base of the skirting.

On a new home, single vertical straps do not require stabilizer plates, but frame straps have a vertical and a diagonal section that should be between 40° and 50°, attaching to the frame and sometimes the next frame if the correct angle cannot be obtained. The stabilizer plate helps to keep the anchor rod from being dragged through the soil. The plates are either hot dipped galvanized or ABS and the top should be flush with the grade.

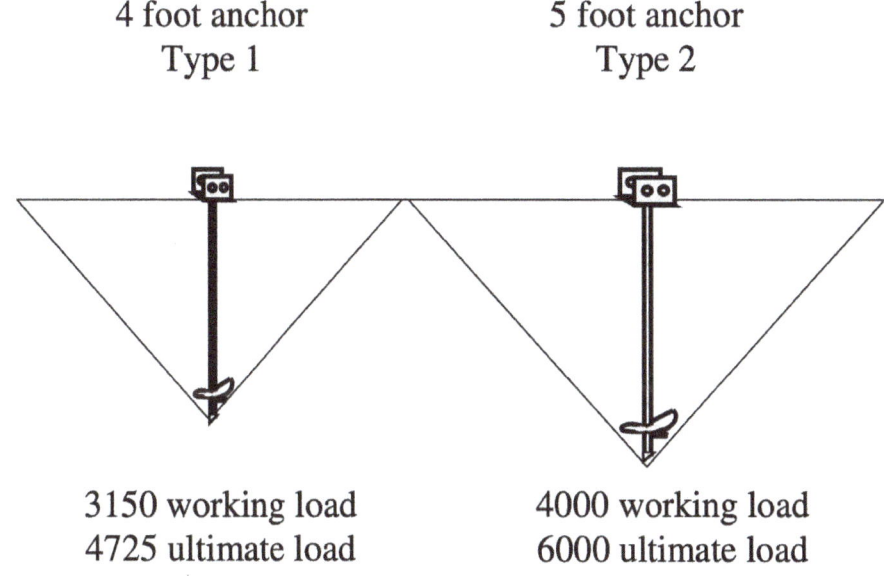

4 foot anchor
Type 1

5 foot anchor
Type 2

3150 working load
4725 ultimate load

4000 working load
6000 ultimate load

Vertical Ties

The three types of vertical ties are sidewall, centerline and shear wall and all help keep the house from overturning in a storm. A proper ground anchor is required at manufacturer-installed straps or brackets. The standard spacing is 5'-4" on center and also within 2-feet of each end. Centerline ties are required for both new and used homes.

Vertical and Frame Straps

All straps should be tight and corrosion-free. The Florida override has specific rules for straps-buckles: wrapping the strap around the I beam, hooks to the I beam (instead of frame clamps) or excess strap wrapped around anchor bolt are not allowed.

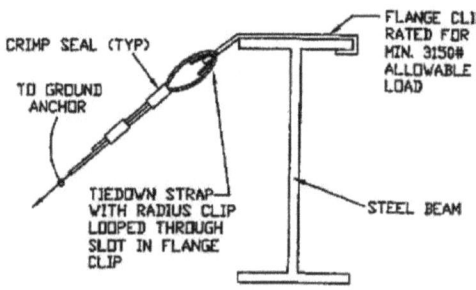

Only frame clamps should be used to connect to I-beam. No hooks.

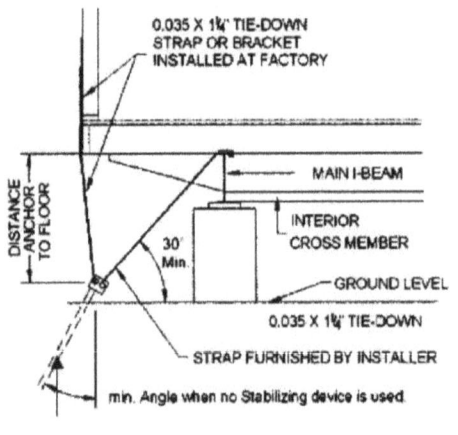

Anchors should not be installed at steep angles.

The Florida override requires that frame clamps be attached to the top of the beam, other states allow attachment at the bottom. Also in Florida frame tie-downs can be spaced at no further than 5'-4" on center with anchors placed within 2-feet of each end.

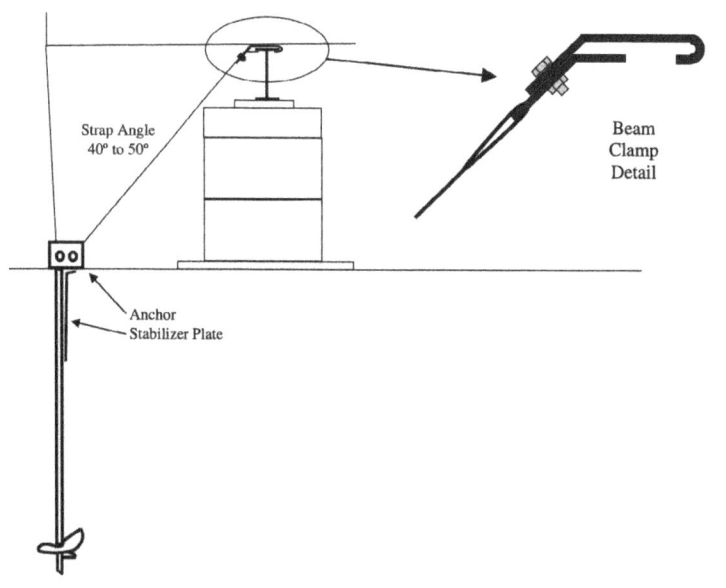

Strap Angle 40° to 50°

Beam Clamp Detail

Anchor
Stabilizer Plate

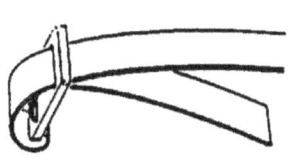

Buckles are not allowed.

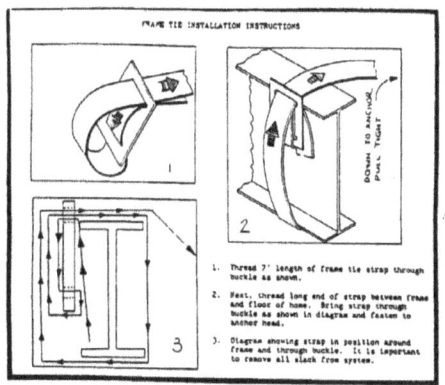

Wrapping the strap around the I-beam is not allowed.

    Any lengthening of a strap requires a 12" strap overlap with two seals and two crimps, both evenly spaced.

    The approved method of connecting to the manufacturer installed brackets or where brackets have been welded to the frame at the sidewall and centerlines is to loop the strap using a crimp seal with two crimps evenly spaced and protected by a radius clip.

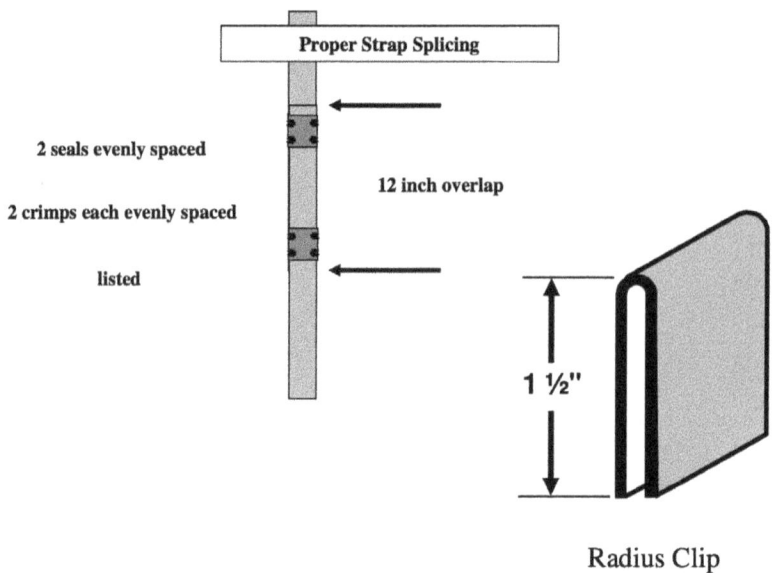

Longitudinal Bracing

Longitudinal bracing is designed to resist horizontal wind loads applied to the ends of the structure and this is where they are located. Strapping with ground anchors and stabilizer plates or longitudinal stabilizing devices are the approved methods of longitudinal bracing, in addition to the anchoring systems for along the side walls and marriage line.

When anchor straps are used they must connect to a factory welded clip on the frame or another device mechanically attached.

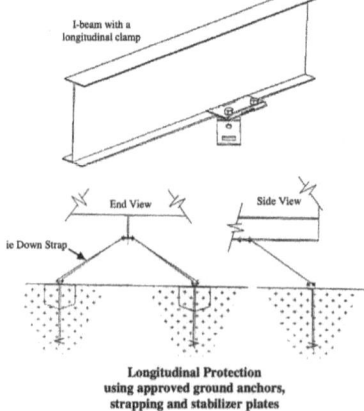

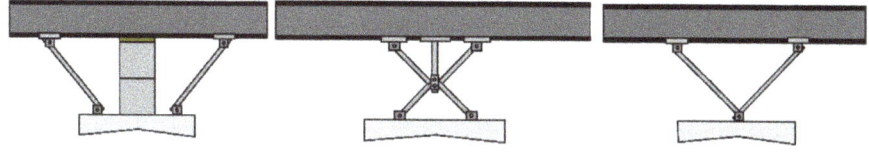

Longitudinal Protection using approved
Longitudinal Stabilizing Devices
(LSDs)

A single wide will have two devices, a double wide four and a triple wide requires six. These systems consist of a galvanized pan anchored in the grade with pins and square galvanized steel tubing that attaches to the frame.

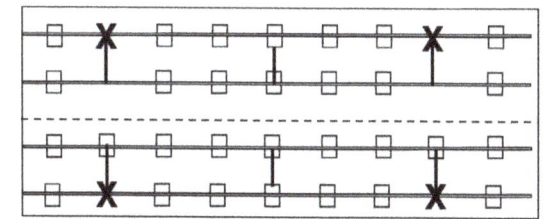

Double wide greater than 52' in length showing four LSDs and 6 lateral arm systems.

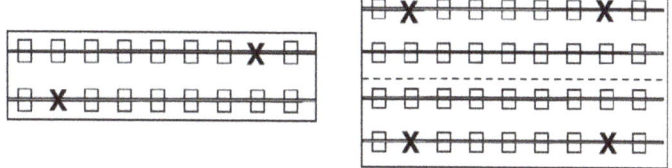

Longitudinal Stabilizing Devices shown on typical blocking plans.

Lateral Arm Systems

Sometimes telescoping lateral arms will share a pad with the longitudinal system and the other end attaching to the top of the far I-beam, although these are separate systems. The use of lateral

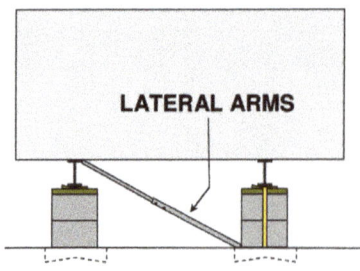

arms requires vertical ties spaced at 5'-4" on center; so if an older home does not have that spacing then lateral arms cannot be used. Four lateral arms are required for homes up to 52-feet in length and six arms for any longer.

Roof Ties

When factory installed roof ties are not evident at homes man-ufactured before July 13, 1994, and it cannot be determined that the mobile/manufactured home is "Hurricane Resistant" without roof ties, then the number of roof ties, as shown by the table below, should be found installed. They should be installed to not have contact with the structure, except at adequately reinforced areas, where additional load will not damage the structure.

1. Single-wide homes less than or equal to 60-feet require three roof ties.

2. Single wide homes greater than or equal to 61-feet require four roof ties.

3. Double wide homes require roof ties only if installed by the manufacturer.

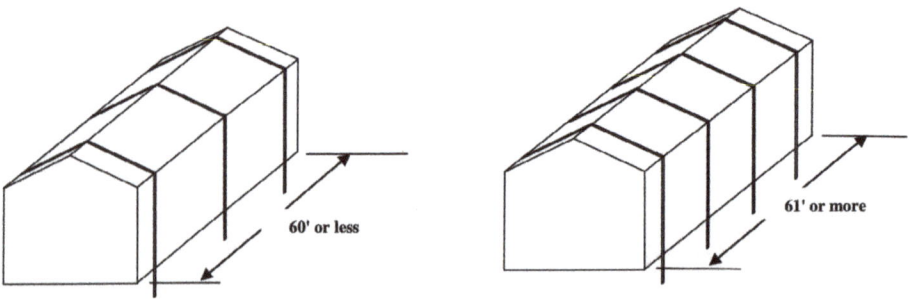

End roof ties or vertical ties should be installed at maximum 24-inches from the end of the structure, or at the first stud and truss, and they should be attached to the same anchor as the frame tie. If the steel frame does not extend to the back end wall, then the roof tie should be installed within 6-inches of the end of the chassis. Intermediate roof ties or vertical ties shall then be located at midway or equally spaced between the end roof ties, as feasible.

All new park models manufactured after January 2, 1995, should have at least three factory installed vertical tie points in addition to the required frame ties.

ANCHORS AND TIE-DOWNS

Twelve or more requirements of proper anchor and tie down installation are required at each vertical/diagonal anchor location.

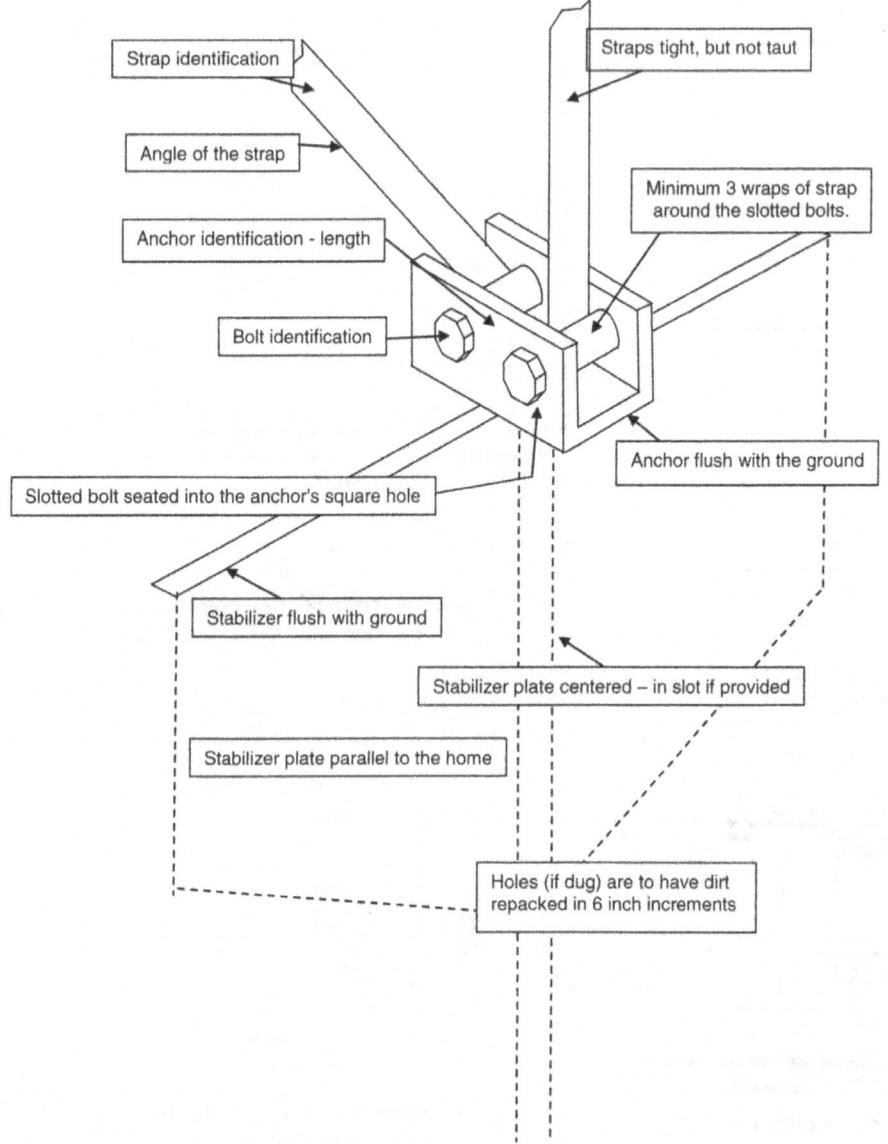

Tie-Down Upgrade Timeline

Here's the effective dates of the upgrades to tie-down requirements for HUD and Florida, along with events that spurred the changes:

1973 - Florida begins requiring tie-downs, at four corners only.

June 15, 1976 - HUD takes control of mobile home standards, and additional tie down requirements added per manufacturer's installation manuals.

August 24, 1992 - Hurricane Andrew strikes South Florida.

July 13, 1994 - HUD upgrades structural requirements, including addition of Wind Zone 3 for high-wind prone hurricane areas of Florida.

October 1, 1996 - Florida begins requiring mobile home installers to be licensed.

February 23, 1998 - Tornados hit Orlando area.

March 29, 1999 - Florida makes major changes to strengthen the tie-down requirements above HUD standards, part of the state Administrative Code Rule 15C-1.

January 1, 2009 - HUD creates a national standard for mobile home installation.

Crawlspace and Tie-Downs Checklist

1) Take a look at the site including neighboring properties to determine how water might flow around or under the home.

2) Locate the entry scuttle, HVAC unit, main plumbing drain and note additions or any other possible crawlspace obstructions.

3) Check skirting for damage, any openings big enough for a small animal to enter, or lack of adequate cross ventilation.

4) Walk through the interior to understand the plumbing layout, large clear openings in the center line walls and also water heater, HVAC and clothes dryer locations.

5) Once in the crawlspace scan for evidence of moisture past or present. A watermark several inches up a pier makes a great defect photo. Look for corrosion on the frame and tie down components. If the house was installed after 10/20/08 there should be a vapor barrier on the soil that covers the entire crawlspace with no openings.

6) Sight down the outside row of piers looking for leaning or damaged piers and incorrect caps or shims. The large exterior openings like sliding glass doors should have supporting piers. If you are in a big, comfortable crawlspace check pier heights and block configurations.

7) Make sure the vertical tie straps at the side walls and center lines are spaced at max. 5'-4" on center for newer homes and older ones with upgraded tied-downs; and there will be another set two feet from each end. Anchor heads and stabilizer plates should be flush with grade. The straps will be attached to the frame mechanically. Look for proper splicing. For frame ties check that the angle is between 40° and 50°.

8) Moving to the center line you can repeat the pier/tie down drill and then begin looking for larger pier configurations and pads at the ends of the large center line wall openings. You should not see a center line or side wall opening of more than 15-feet without increased bearing of concrete or plastic pads.

10) While checking the belly board for bulging, damage or temporary repairs keep an eye open for clothes dryer ducts terminating in the crawlspace, condensate from HVAC systems or a water heater with a failing T&P valve and supply/drain piping leaks.

11) There are components for the HVAC and plumbing sections of your inspection in the crawlspace to check before you leave.

Belly Board and Vapor Barrier

Exposed wood floor framing and floor sheathing close to the ground will start to rot if humid, stagnant air collects under a manufactured home. So a continuous plastic sheet, called a "belly board," seals the underside of the home, and a plastic vapor barrier must be installed over the ground to eliminate evaporating moisture rising up into the air in the crawl space.

The belly board has been required for many years, so you should expect an intact belly board under any manufactured home. But a vapor barrier covering the ground in the crawl space, although recommended for years, did not become a HUD-code requirement for home installations until October 20, 2008. The entire area beneath the home should be covered, except for under porches, decks, and recessed entries.

The plastic sheeting must be minimum 6-mil thick, with 12" or more overlaps, and can be placed under, over, or around footings at grade. An exception is for allowed homes installed in an area of dry soils.

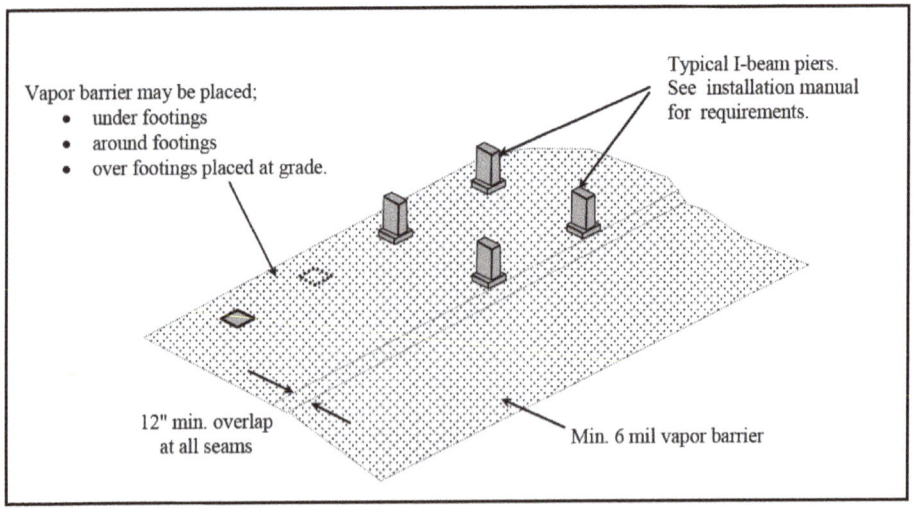

The belly board must be continuous, with no openings, over the entire underside of the home. A common defect is a ragged, torn opening under the kitchen or bathroom where a plumbing repair was made, but the belly board was not resealed. Besides allowing moisture into the floor framing, it also exposes insulation that dangles down within reach of any critters that may get through an opening in the skirting. Raccoons love to have a party pulling down all the insulation and belly board plastic once an opening has been started.

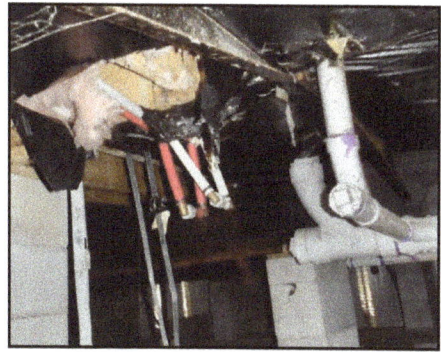

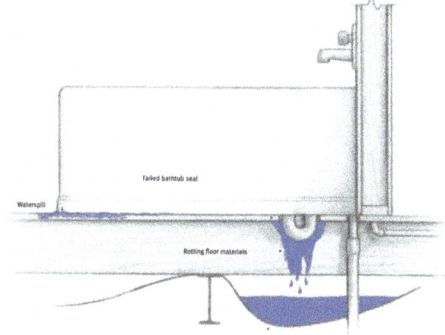

Water leakage under a plumbing fixture can cause a sag in the belly board. Belly boards tend to sag a little over time anyway, but an excessive sag may indicate a problem. Push up on the bulging area with the palm of your hand. If it feels heavy, prick it with a knife point to check for water above.

Belly Board and Vapor Barrier Checklist

1) Verify the presence of a vapor barrier, unless the home was installed before October 20, 2008. Note any damage.

2) Document any openings in the belly board. Test any sagging areas for water accumulation.

Florida Overrides

Florida has frequent hurricanes, sandy soil, and a hot/humid climate. Although any one of those factors does not make the state unique, the combination of all three does. Yet Florida abided by the same HUD national standards for manufactured homes as all the other states across the U.S. from the time they became law in 1976.

Then Hurricane Andrew swept across South Florida in 1991. Just about all the mobile homes in the hardest-hit areas around Homestead, near the southern tip of the state, were knocked off their foundation piers and ripped apart by the storm. HUD responded by creating a new Wind Zone 3 just for us several years later in 1994, with tougher wind-resistant standards for South Florida.

But the state determined that installation standards that exceeded HUD guidelines were necessary for safe occupancy of a manufactured home. So Chapters 15C-1 and 15C-2 of the Florida Administrative Code were created in 1999. The regulations are enforced by the Manufactured Housing Section of the Florida Department of Highway Safety and Motor Vehicles.

The following are some examples of the state's stricter installation rules, which are often referred to as "Florida overrides". But the first three are the ones likely to affect a home inspection:

•• Minimum height from ground to bottom of frame I-beam is 18-inches, except that 25% of area can be lower, but not below 12-inches clearance. HUD allows lower.

•• Frame clamps for straps must be attached to the top of I-beam. HUD allows attachment to the bottom.

•• Piers are required near each end of the home's centerline, whether or not the manufacturer requires them.

•• Wood foundations are not allowed.

•• Tie-down straps must be double-dip (0.60 oz. per sq. ft.) galvanized. HUD allows 0.30 oz. per sq. ft.

•• Piers over 52-inches high must be engineered. HUD accepts up to 80-inches before engineering necessary.

For the full text of the Florida Overrides, go to:
https://www.flrules.org/gateway/organization.asp?id=42
and then select 15C-1 and 15C-2

Pit Set

When a manufactured home is installed very close to ground level, making it look more like a site-built home, it has a "pit set" foundation. Because access to the bottom structure of the mobile home is necessary for maintenance and ventilation, a shallow pit must be dug under the footprint of the home. Then a structural stem wall is built following the shape of the perimeter of the home. It provides support under the exterior walls and also acts as a retaining wall to keep the surrounding soil from migrating back into the pit over time. Interior stacked block piers on pads along the marriage line and at support points for the steel beams are still necessary, the same as in a regular installation.

We have inspected only a few pit set homes in our North Central Florida area over the past decade and, unfortunately, have found that they are not well suited for sites where the water table rises close to the ground during the wet season. The result is a house over a mucky pond for part of the year. One pit set that we inspected was a foreclosure, mold-filled and abandoned by the owner—the result of an especially long and wet rainy season that the home spent sitting over standing water. But, when sited correctly, a pit set can be a good alternative for a manufactured home installation.

A pit set installation is more expensive—and requires more engineering—than a standard, elevated installation that uses only the economical, stacked block piers on pads and plastic skirting. To learn more about pit set foundations, we suggest visiting the website of Harrison Engineering LLC, a company that specializes in providing foundation plans for manufactured homes nationwide, at www.mobilehomefoundation.com.

Roofs

Before the mid-1970s mobile home roofs were flat, or more accurately very shallow pitched, roofs sheathed in metal panels or a roofing mem-
brane. Of course low-pitch roofs have more problems over time than a higher pitch, so the industry raised the pitch and newer homes look more like a site-built. But one of the pluses of inspecting mobile homes is skipping the attic crawl on a hot summer afternoon.

The roofing material on a new manufactured/mobile home, along with the fastening method, has been approved by HUD as part of the overall design approval based on the wind zone for which the home is rated. But, when it is time to replace the roof, it is not longer subject to HUD standards.

Any roof replacement is under the jurisdiction of the local building department, and the requirements are the same as for a site-built home, with one exception: a roof-over (installing the new roof directly over an old roof without removing it) is not allowed for asphalt shingles. The roof structure of a mobile home is not designed to withstand the weight of two layers of shingle roofing. But a metal roof-over is allowed.

Asphalt shingles weigh between 2 and 3 pounds per square foot, depending on the quality of the shingle, so a roof recover on a 2,000 square foot doublewide would add 2 to 3 tons of weight on the roof. A roof-over with metal is significantly lighter, and allowed, but an asphalt shingle roof must be stripped off and a new underlayment applied before installing new asphalt shingles.

There are few differences between a mobile home roof and a site built home, but you will notice different roof penetration coverings such as a string of small pan-covered roof vents and plumbing vents with hoods.

Skylights can be problematic on mobile home roofs. Two factors cause mobile home skylights to have a higher-than-average incidence of leakage than site-built homes: 1) many of them do not have a raised frame or curb, and 2) mobile home roofs usually have a lower roof slope than site-built homes.

The raised perimeter and proper, down-lapped installation is important, especially on a lower slope roof. Above right is an example of a better quality skylight and installation, one that is obviously more expensive.

Roof Checklist

1) Are all secondary roofs flashed properly between slopes and wall junctions? Most site built additions have numerous reportable defects and some that we have seen over the years ignore the principle of downlapping.

2) Are the shingles secured at the drip edge? Is tab adhesion a problem? How is granule loss, pitting?

3) Are there dissimilar metals in contact with one another for metal roofs? This can cause galvanic corrosion in coastal areas.

4) Are panels installed per manufacturers specs: screw spacing and placement, less than 1-inch of panel overhanging drip edge, male flange on the bottom and female on top? Is there properly installed trim at the gable ends? Is ridge cap secured?

5) Are all roof penetrations including skylights correctly installed and in good condition?

6) Are there elastomeric coatings across the roof or temporary repairs with mastic?

Additions

A question we get often is: "Does an addition to a mobile home have to meet HUD code?" And the answer is no, an addition only has to comply with local building code for site-built structures.

But the wall of a mobile is only engineered to support itself and nothing more, so an addition cannot bear on the wall of the home. Florida Administrative Code Rule 15C-2.0081 states that *"additions, including, but not limited to add-a-rooms, roof-overs and porches shall be free standing and self-supporting with only the flashing attached to the main unit unless the added unit has been designed to be married to the existing unit. All additions shall be constructed in compliance with State and locally adopted building codes."* Other states have similar standards. An example of the correct way to do an addition is shown below, where the addition is bearing on posts and a beam next to the home.

An exception to the requirement that an addition not bear, or be directly connected to, a manufactured home is allowed when the manufacturer installs a "host beam" in the wall where the connection of the site-built addition will be made, and beefs up both the pier and tie-down specs for the area below the connection.

This upgrade should be noted in the Performance Certificate (data plate). If not, verification would require contacting the manufacturer—which is outside the scope on an inspection. But, if there is an addition bearing on the walls of the home, we suggest recommending that the buyer request that the information be provided by the seller or contact the manufacturer directly for it.

There is also a second reason for this requirement in hurricane-prone states like Florida. An aluminum screen porch or carport is often attached to the fascia of the home, and it will pull off the fascia when a hurricane blows the aluminum addition away. The missing fascia depressurizes the home interior and allows the wind to get under the sheathing; and then part, or all, of the home's roof comes off next.

Performance Certificate

The HUD Performance Certificate is a paper sticker attached to an interior surface of the home. It's often referred to as the "data plate" and provides the home's construction specifications. It has been required by HUD since they took over the supervision of manufactured home construction in June, 1976.

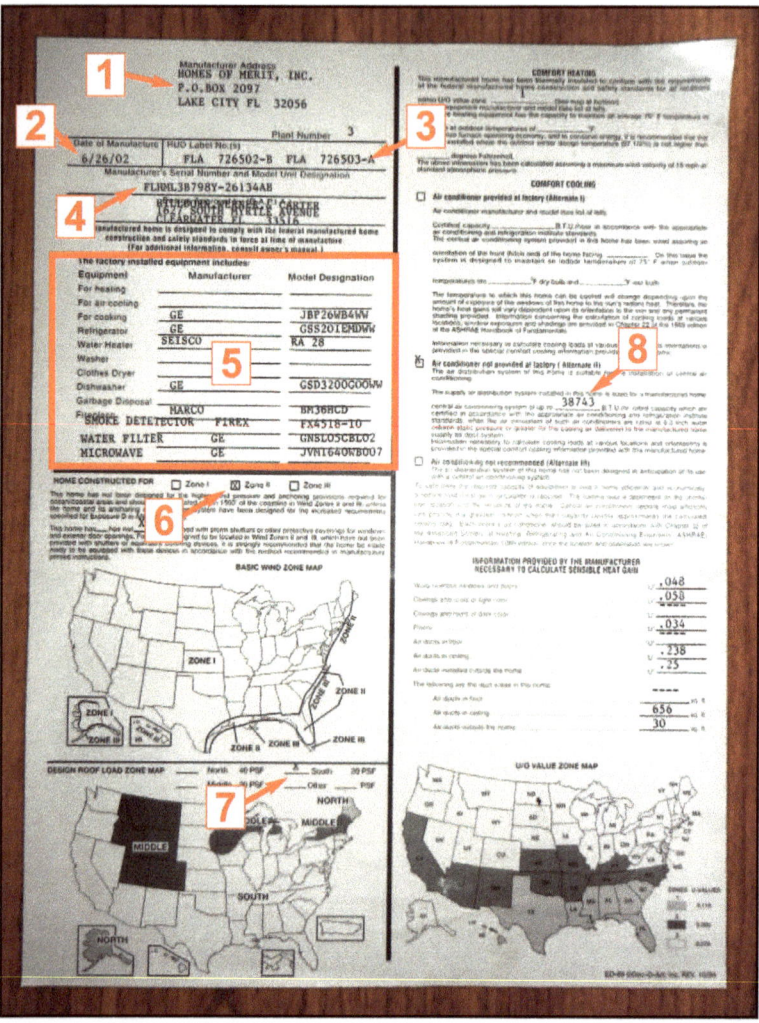

The data plate is usually found in one of these four locations: 1) wall of the master bedroom closet, 2) back of one of the kitchen cabinet doors, 3) side wall of the base cabinet under the kitchen sink, or 4) back of a hinged wood door covering the electric panel.

Here's an outline of the data you can retrieve and where to find it:

1. The name of the manufacturer and the location of the factory where it was produced.

2. The date of manufacture. The year of manufacture is important, because construction standards were strengthened over the years, especially after certain key dates. Between June, 1976, (beginning of HUD Code) and July, 1994, all mobile homes were required to meet a single minimum standard. HUD has raised the standards several times since then. See page 31 for more on this.

3. A listing of the certification label numbers (also called HUD tag numbers) affixed to each transportable section of the home. One number for a single-wide, two for a double-wide, and so forth. They should match the numbers found on the metal tags riveted to the outside wall of the home.

4. The manufacturer's serial number and model designation of the home. In some versions of the data plate, the model designation is in a separate box.

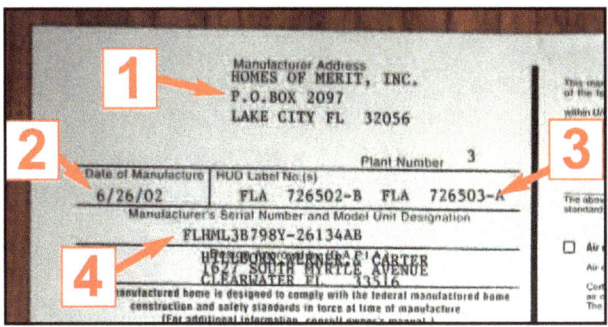

5. A list of the factory-installed equipment, including the manufacturer's name and model number. Comparing this list with the refrigerator, range, water heater, and other currently installed appliances in the home will tell you whether they are original to the construction or newer.

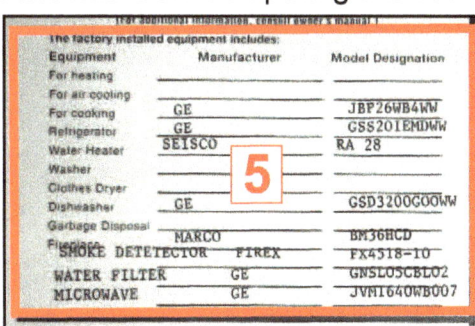

45

6. **A check-box for the "wind load zone" in which the home was designed to be located.** Zones are I, II, and III—with II and III zones constructed to withstand hurricane-force winds. Zone 3 is for the higher hurricane winds in South Florida and southeastern coastal areas. Here too, compare the wind load zone checked with the adjacent map to verify proper construction for the where the home is located. A home designed for a higher number wind zone can be located in a lower zone, but a number lower than the zone of the location is not acceptable. Also, there is no Zone I in Florida, so a Zone I home cannot be moved to Florida

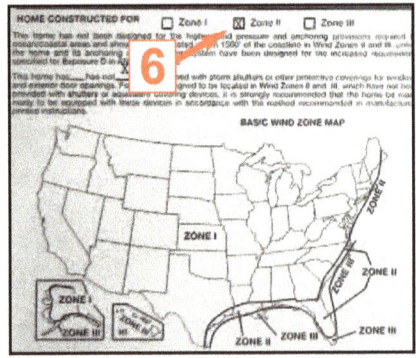

7. **A check-box for the "roof load zone" in which the home was designed to be located.** Northern roof load zones are meant to allow for a snow load. Compare the roof load zone checked with the adjacent small U.S. map to confirm that the home meets the standard for where it is located.

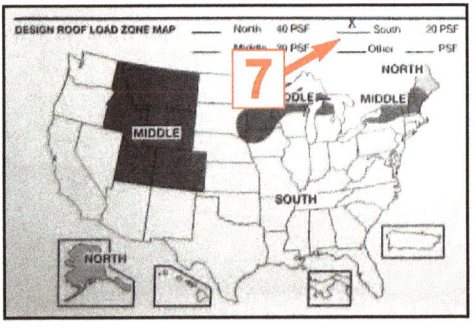

8. **Heating and cooling data and "thermal map."** This shows the zone the home was designed to be located in, along with a calculation of the level of heat transmission of the building envelope. Sometimes this is a separate plate. A home designed for a higher number thermal zone can be located in a lower zone, but not vice-versa.

What heating or cooling equipment was factory-installed in the home is also noted, with BTU rating. If no cooling system was factory installed, a recommended size unit is stated in BTUs. It is stated as "up to," meaning the number is a recommended maximum. Some homeowners replace their old air conditioner with one far above the BTUs of the manufacturer's recommendation, which can cause moisture problems in the home. So it's worth noting in your report when you see a significantly oversized air conditioner.

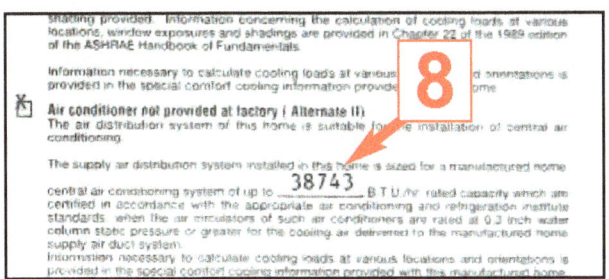

The rating of the home's insulation is in U-value, which many homebuyers are unfamiliar with. To present the insulation data, if requested, we recommend converting to the more familiar R-value, which is the multiplication inverse of U-values. So a U-value of .058 is 1 ÷ .058 = 17.

Unfortunately, the data plate is often missing in older homes. If the homebuyer needs any of the data plate info for financing or insurance, it can be retrieved from IBTS (Institute for Business and Tecnology Safety) by filing a request at their website at www.ibts.org. You will need to give them the HUD tag number or serial number and pay a fee to receive it. See page 65 to learn more.

Wind Zones

There are three HUD wind zones, numbered 1, 2, and 3, plus an additional "Exposure D" zone for homes in zones 2 and 3 that are within 1500 feet of the coastline, where there are often higher wind speeds and the possibility of storm surge across the foundation. The wind zone standard the home was designed to meet can be verified at the Performance Certificate inside the home, and should be checked for where the home is sited. See page 44 for more about Performance Certificates.

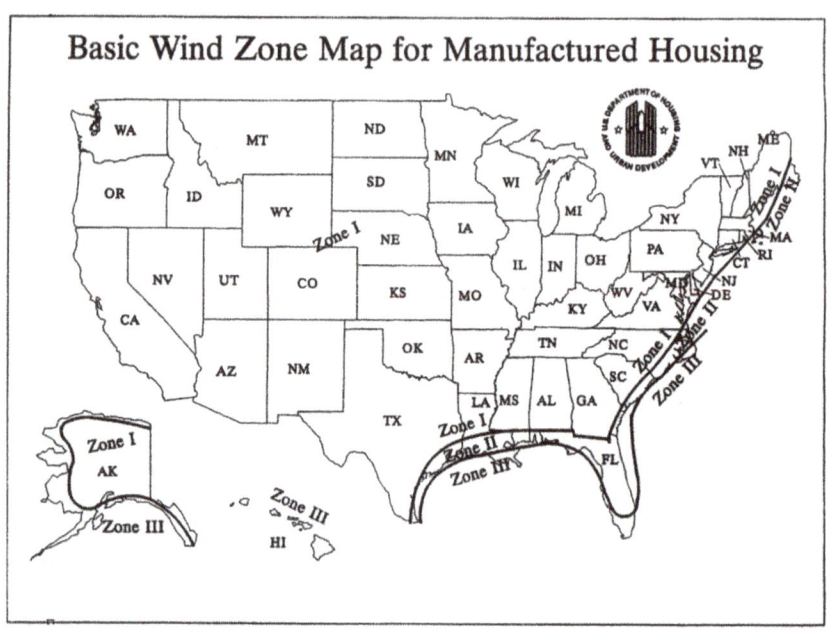

Zone 1 means the home was built for a location that is not expected to be exposed to hurricanes. Zone 2 means the home was designed for installation in an area prone to hurricanes with maximum sustained winds of up to 100 mph. And Zone 3 is for homes located in areas that can expect hurricane winds over 100 mph, which is primarily South Florida and a few areas along the Gulf Coast.

No part of Florida is within Zone 1, so a Zone 1 home cannot be moved to Florida. Also, HUD interprets Exposure D to be for just the coastline, and it does not include the inland shoreline of bays, lakes, or rivers.

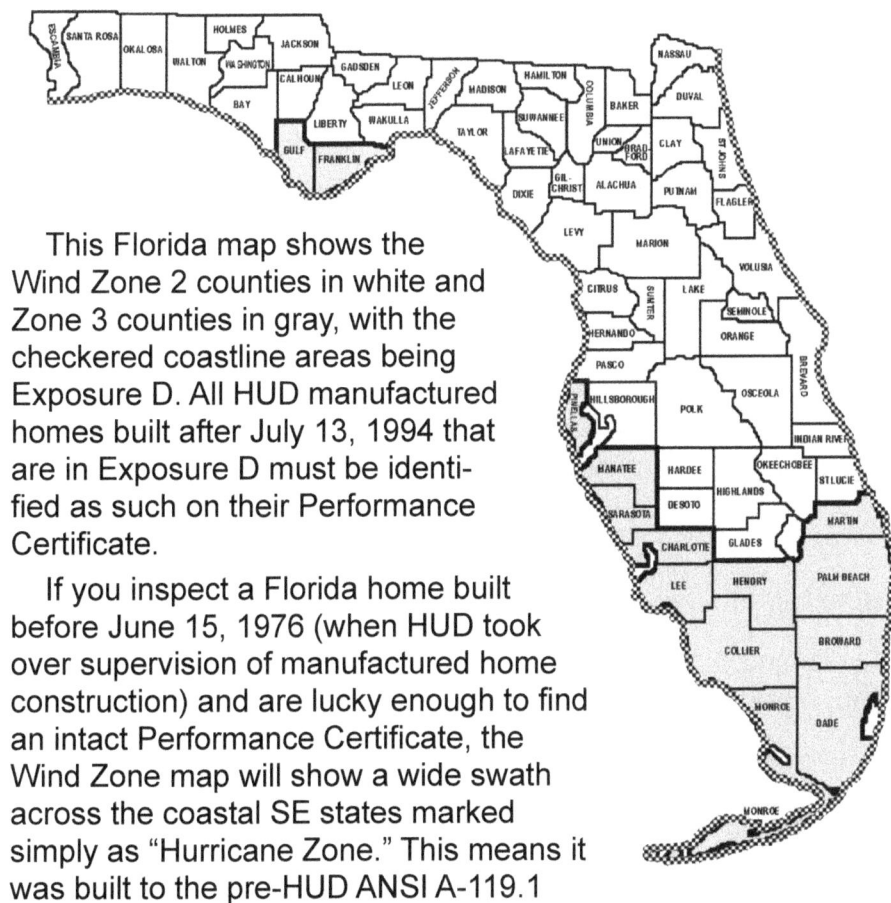

This Florida map shows the Wind Zone 2 counties in white and Zone 3 counties in gray, with the checkered coastline areas being Exposure D. All HUD manufactured homes built after July 13, 1994 that are in Exposure D must be identified as such on their Performance Certificate.

If you inspect a Florida home built before June 15, 1976 (when HUD took over supervision of manufactured home construction) and are lucky enough to find an intact Performance Certificate, the Wind Zone map will show a wide swath across the coastal SE states marked simply as "Hurricane Zone." This means it was built to the pre-HUD ANSI A-119.1 standard.

Homes built between June 15, 1976 and July 13, 1994, will show all of Florida as in Wind Zone 2. Hurricane Andrew, that walloped South Florida in 1992 with 160 mph winds, was the impetus for the upgrade in wind resistance standards with the addition of Wind Zone 3 two years later.

Although HUD has jurisdiction over the manufacture and installation standards for manufactured homes, local code standards for wind resistance will apply for any carports, additions, utility buildings, driveways or steps at the home. In Florida, that means that the Florida Building Code and Wind Zone Map applies.

Crowned Floors

A crowned floor sags along the long walls and has a shallow hump at the marriage line of a double-wide or center line of a single-wide. This is typically caused by homes that have no perimeter piers or not enough of them, especially older ones, or at locations of concentrated loads. The problem can be felt by walking across the floor, or by observing a slight tilt of furniture. It occurs gradually over time, eventually causing problems.

Here's a list of other possible symptoms:

- Uneven floors.

- Doors and windows difficult to open

- Drooping of roof near long exterior walls or at the ridge

- Buckling or racking of interior wallboard panels.

- Loosening of the connection between the walls and the floor or ceiling.

Anything that adds more weight at the long walls will make the crown worse, such as heavy furniture, appliances, or snow buildup on the roof.

The two steel I-beams that provide the main support of a mobile home are parallel to the long walls of each unit of the home, but inset several feet from the walls. The floor joists that sit on top of the beams run perpendicular to them, and are cantilevered as they extend past the beam. In other words, they are unsupported where they end under the long walls.

The long walls push down on the end of that cantilever with a combination of the weight of the wall itself, the area of roof bearing on the wall, and any additional loads next to the wall such as a bathtub. Also, any large openings in the wall, like a sliding glass door or double-window, transfer the roof weight over them via a header to both sides of the opening, creating a concentrated load at these locations on the wall.

The diagram below helps explain the situation. Think of the bearing point at the chassis I-beam (blue arrow) as the center of a see-saw, with lots of weight on side "A," and not much weight at side "B." As the unsupported end of the joists at "A" begins to sag downward under the heavy load, the "B" side responds by bowing upward. This creates a "crown," or hump in the center of the floor.

Mobile home manufacturers overcome this problem by requiring piers at specific locations under these walls. They are called "perimeter" or "sidewall" piers to distinguish them from the piers that support the steel chassis. Although piers are needed along the walls and marriage line for a general load, typical locations for additional sidewall piers are places where there is a concentrated load, like a fireplace, inset porch, and where kitchen cabinets run along the wall—besides under the sides of sliding glass doors or large windows already mentioned.

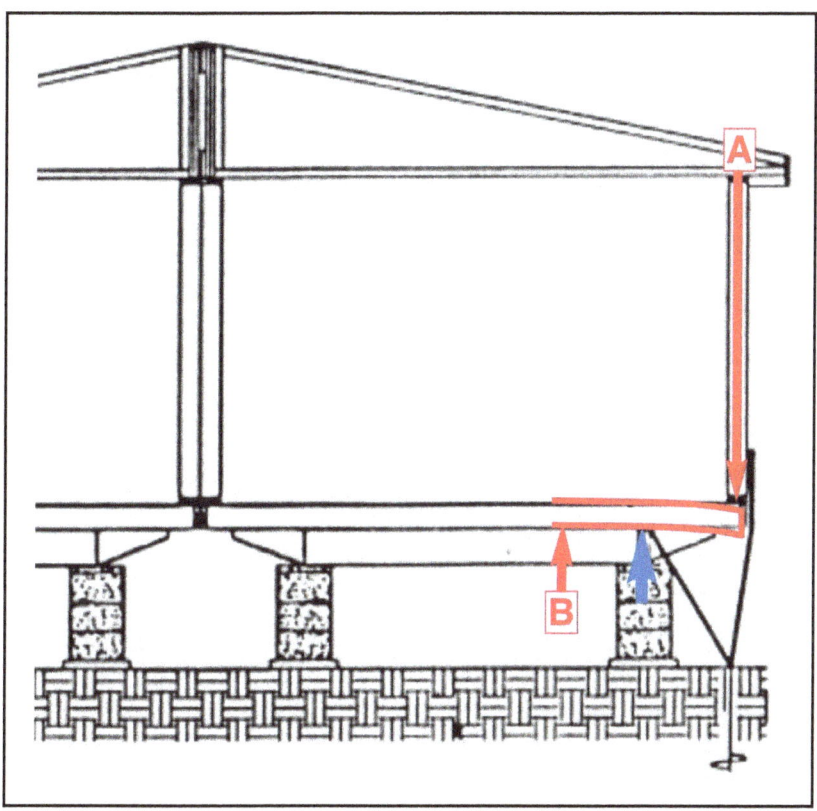

The photo above shows a single-wide on a dealer lot. Because the long sides are not supported until installation at the homesite, it's easier to see the kind of sagging that occurs when there is not enough or uneven support along the long side. Although in this case it is only temporary.

The fix for this problem requires a professional mobile home installer. It is not a simple job that a homeowner can tackle successfully. Bringing the piers under the exterior walls and marriage line into alignment at the same level fixes the crown, but can throw the bearing at the piers under the I-beams of the chassis out of whack. Some bearing points at the I-beams may end up sitting above the piers until they "relax" back down, and a second adjustment could be necessary. An experienced, professional installer knows how far things can be pushed without causing damage, especially if the floor has been crowned for while.

Plumbing

The HUD requirements for manufactured home plumbing are at 24 CFR 3280.601, but they are essentially the same as site-built home plumbing code. Connection of the system to the water supply and septic tank or sewer is under the jurisdiction of the local building code.

But many manufacturers used polybutylene (PB) water supply piping during the 1980s and '90s, until the leakage problems and lawsuits caused the piping to lose code approval. Most homes will already have replaced their PB due to leakage or the difficulty in getting homeowners insurance because of it.

Then there's cross-linked polyethylene (PEX), the "new and improved" version of PB, which has been used in new homes and replacement piping for PB. It has had similar problems as it aged, and many insurors now decline coverage for homes with PEX pipe manufactured before 2011. Pipe produced later was reformulated to be more heat resistant.

Otherwise, manufactured homes almost always arrive from the factory with plumbing in good condition and satisfactory. Most problems occur later with homeowner repairs. Defects that are not allowed by the HUD code or site-built codes are what to look for: like saddle-tap valves, double-trap at sink, and unrated accordion-type pipe used for sink tailpiece, for example. Also, damage to belly board and insulation under the floor at plumbing repair in crawl space.

53

Water Heaters

All mobile home manufacturers put the water heater in a compartment with an access panel secured with screws. Older mobile homes have the access panel on an outside wall, usually next to a bathroom or kitchen window. Also, there may be an on/off switch in or near the bathroom that must be turned-on for testing, and some switches glow red to indicate when the water heater is on.

Newer mobile homes locate the water heater compartment access panel in the master bedroom closet or laundry. The raised panel with a narrow trim piece around it is easy to recognize, and the screws typically each have a snap-off cover to conceal the screw head.

If you have tried looking in these locations and still can't find the water heater, here are several other possibilities:

1) Sometimes a homeowner or remodeler installs new siding on an older mobile home and sides right over the access panel, making it disappear. Yes, it's silly, but it does happen.

2) When a long-term leak in the water heater compartment rots out the floor, some ingenious homeowners put a low-boy water heater on the ground directly under the compartment. Check in the crawl space.

3) If the homeowner decided to upgrade to a larger water heater that does not fit in the compartment, it may have been moved to a shed on the ground next to the exterior wall of the compartment, or to a detached shed, carport storage room, or even a well house.

4) If the water heater has been on for a while, an infrared camera can help you find it.

Only water heaters that meet the published standards of the U.S. Department of Housing and Urban Development (HUD) under Title 24 CFR Part 3280, "Manufactured Home Construction and Safety Standards," are allowed by HUD to be installed in NEW mobile homes. They have the following characteristics.

1) Side-plumbed for cold and hot water. This is the easiest way to identify a HUD water heater at a glance.
2) Must have a non-adjustable temperature and pressure relief (TPR) valve.
3) A corrosion resistant catch pan and drain to the exterior necessary under the water heater.
4) Water heater required to be secured in place, usually by a strap system.
5) Approved by a major national rating agency as compliant with HUD standards for energy efficiency.

HUD-approved water heaters will also have a sticker like the one below. Every major water heater manufacturer has models of water heaters specifically designed for mobile homes.

Two requirements that have long been a part of the building code for site-built homes were not included by HUD until about 20 years ago: they did not require a cold water shut-off valve or that the TPR valve piping extend to a visible exterior location. The pipe often terminated straight down below the home in the crawl space.

After a mobile home leaves the factory and is installed at a site, it is no longer under the oversight of HUD. So, a replacement water heater does not have to be approved in most areas. State of California, for example, specifically states that a replacement water heater does not have to be HUD approved.

To avoid the possibility of carbon monoxide leakage into a mobile home when a gas water heater is installed, there must be a complete separation of the combustion system from the interior air of the home. This can be achieved by a "direct vent" sealed combustion system (although not all direct vent water heaters are HUD-approved, so check for a HUD approval sticker) or by a water heater in a compartment that is sealed-off from the living area of the home and only accessible from outside.

Water Heater Checklist

•• Don't be surprised if you find a mess when you open the water heater compartment: an ancient water heater, original to the construction of the home, corroded around the base, with a slow leak and water damage to the sagging floor below it. The water heater is not visible without removing multiple screws, so many homeowners don't check the compartment until it stops functioning.

•• Because older homes were allowed to terminate the TPR discharge pipe below the home, where a leak is not readily visible, you may find a puddle in the crawl space from a continuous, slow hot water leak from a TPR valve failure.

** Older mobile homes were not required to have a cold water shut-off valve, or a catch pan and drain, and the drain termination did not have to be in a readily visible location. But, if the original water heater has been replaced, it should have them.

Emergency Egress

Doors - min. 2 exterior doors for emergency egress, max. 12 feet apart single-wide, and 20 feet apart double-wide. One of doors must be max. 35 feet from door of each bedroom. Travel cannot require passage thru lockable interior door.

Door must have a minimum 28-inch by 72-inch clear opening. Sliding glass door acceptable.

Stairs - required at each exit door, min. full width of door opening, and compliant with local code. See page 11.

Bedroom Windows - must be at min. 22 inches in the horizontal or vertical least dimension and at least five square feet in area, the bottom of the window opening be not more than 36 inches above the floor, and the locks and latches which need to be operated to permit exiting not be located more than 54 inches above the finished floor. The five square feet must be a clear open area, and it must open directly to the exterior. Also, there is an exemption if the sleeping room has a HUD-code exterior door.

All homes leave the factory meeting these emergency exit safety standards, but they are often voided by homeowner remodeling and additions.

Smoke Alarms/Detectors

A smoke detector must be installed on any wall in the hallway or living area outside each sleeping room, and also in each sleeping room. Homes with bedroom areas that are separated require a smoke alarm for each area. They must be interconnected.

The smoke alarms may be wired to house power with a battery backup, or alarms with a 10-year battery only are an acceptable alterative. Also, combination smoke and CO (carbon monoxide) alarms are allowed.

Formerly, a smoke alarm was only required in each hall or area outside each bedroom, and they were hard-wired without a battery backup.

Electrical

The electrical inspection of a manufactured home is the essentially same as a site-built home, with just a few exceptions. First, be *very* careful in calling out electrical defects in newer manufactured homes, and the reason is simple: the HUD code [3280.801(a)] states that  manufactured homes are built to the 2005 edition of the National Electrical Code (NEC). We checked recently, and it is still that way in the 2023 revision of the HUD-code. So, for example, there are all sorts of additional GFCI location requirements updated in each NEC edition since 2005 that do not apply when checking electrical outlets and circuit breakers in a manufactured home.

There also are requirements specific to manufactured homes in Part II of Article 550 of the 2005 NEC. But, even then, HUD states [3280.801(b)] that whenever there is a conflict between the two codes, the HUD-code applies. Although arc-fault breakers began being mandated for bedrooms in the 2002 NEC edition, HUD-code specifically exempts manufactured homes from them [3280.801(b)]. But it does specify that, if arc-fault breakers are installed by the manufacturer, they must meet 2005 NEC standards.

Also, no aluminum wiring, including NEC-approved multi-strand type aluminum, is allowed for branch circuits as part of the original construction of manufactured homes [3280.801(e)].

So, with that out of the way, let's talk about manufactured home electrical systems. There are always at least two electrical panels: a service panel installed at the site, and a distribution subpanel installed inside the home by the manufacturer.

The service panel is not allowed to be attached to, or installed in, a mobile home, with an exception allowed only if the panel meets all seven requirements in NEC 550.32(B).

The panel must be located within sight of the home and not more than 30 feet away. It is typically mounted on a service pole (for overhead service) or service pedestal (for underground service), and the panel must be at least 100 amps and not less than the rating of the manufacturer-installed distribution panel inside the home.

The distribution subpanel is typically located in the laundry or master bedroom. It may be inside a closet in older homes, although that is not allowed today. Like any sub-panel, the neutral wires in the box cannot be on the same bonded bus bar as the grounds. They must be on a separate bus bar that is not bonded.

Most of the electrical defects you will find are due to home-owner remodeling, additions, or deterioration of older electrical components. The original factory-installed electrical systems very rarely have any problems, except for the occasional pre-HUD home built in the early 1970s with solid aluminum branch circuit wiring. Yes, a few of them are still around.

Common Electrical Defects:

1) NM-cables running unprotected or not secured, and across the ground in the crawl space.

2) Service pole leaning significantly out-of-plumb.

3) Unprotected NM-cables around home or in the yard.

4) Wall receptacles loose, damaged, missing face plate, mounted forward of box without a sleeve where wood paneling or kitchen backsplash tile has been added.

5) Severe corrosion at service panel on pole in yard due to long-term water intrusion.

HVAC Systems

HUD requires that a manufactured home have a whole-house ventilation system with a minimum capacity of 0.035 cubic feet per minute per square foot of floor area. The system must have a manual control that is labeled "WHOLE-HOUSE VENTILATION," and cannot draw or exhaust air from the crawl space, floor, wall, or ceiling/roof assemblies. The ventilation system can be part of the home's heating and cooling system, but must be capable of being operated separately.

The whole-house ventilation requirements are typically met by manufacturers with a small, low volume fan behind a grille in the ceiling of a hallway that exhausts out the roof or a fresh-air intake duct from the roof that connects to the return air plenum of the furnace or air handler. The requirement that it be able to be operated separately is fulfilled by setting the air handler fan at "ON" at the thermostat if the heating/cooling system is off.

Although older homes may have only an electric or gas furnace in a compartment within the home and not central air conditioning, newer homes often have a package unit heat pump or package unit air conditioner with an electric resistance heat strip.

HVAC Checklist

1) How does the BTU rating of the air conditioning compare with the recommended maximum listed on the performance certificate (data plate)? If it is significantly more than the recommended maximum, such as a 5-ton unit serving a home with a HUD-recommended 3-ton maximum, it will likely have—or soon develop— moisture issues due lack of sufficient running time for dehumidifying the air.

2) Are the main supply and return air ducts for a package unit hung above the ground? HUD-code does not allow ducts sitting on the ground.

Termites

Both subterranean and drywood termites can infest a mobile home in the warmer parts of the country. Termites enter a mobile in the same way that they would access a site-built structure. Subterranean termites utilize wood-to-earth contact or build mud tubes up the foundation. Drywood termites enter by flying through a small opening in the exterior or in infested wood furniture brought into the home.

So it's important to look carefully for mud tubes when under the home, and small piles of termite fecal pellets (frass) on the floor or damaged wood with termite galleries when inside. Here's an example of a subterranean termite mud tube climbing up a pier into a mobile home.

Mobile homes tend to have more moisture intrusion issues as they age compared to site built homes and wet wood is a favorite for termites. The "belly wrap" vapor barrier that covers the underside of the floor framing on a mobile home can obscure the view of evidence and damage from termites and easily retain moisture from plumbing leaks.

Termite Checklist

1) Is there any wood in the crawlspace in contact with the ground that also connects with the underside of the home? This would provide a way for subterraneans to crawl up to the wood framing undetected.

2) Is there wood stored on the ground under the home, which will attract termites?

3) Look for any wrinkling or deformation of the surface of wood trim inside or outside the home. Gently probe any areas you find. If termite galleries are underneath, the surface will crumble. If the wood crumbles, but no galleries, it may be wood rot.

61

Park Models

A park model is a smaller, single-wide mobile home that is classified as a recreational vehicle. Park models are designed for placement in RV parks, campgrounds, or locations where smaller trailers are allowed; but, like an RV, cannot be a living unit on private property in most jurisdictions.

They are typically 10 or 12 feet wide and have just one bedroom. Although classified as an RV, park models are not intended to be readily moveable, and are often used as a seasonal residence. They were formerly called "park trailers", but the name was upgraded to park model years ago.

Most park models are built under the American National Standards Institute's ANSI-119.5 standard, and are 400 square foot maximum. But that is raised to 500 square feet, in Florida only, when the unit is built to HUD standards for RV park models. These larger Florida park models will have a HUD data plate and HUD tag.

ANSI park models have a basic data plate on an interior wall, usually at or near the electric panel, and it includes the name and address of the manufacturer, date of manufacture, serial or VIN number, and a statement that the unit was built in compliance with ANSI 119.5.

HUD park models have a standard data plate (performance certificate). Although they are manufactured under the same HUD standards as regular mobile homes, which have a minimum size of 400 square feet, some mobile home parks will not allow park models because of their small size.

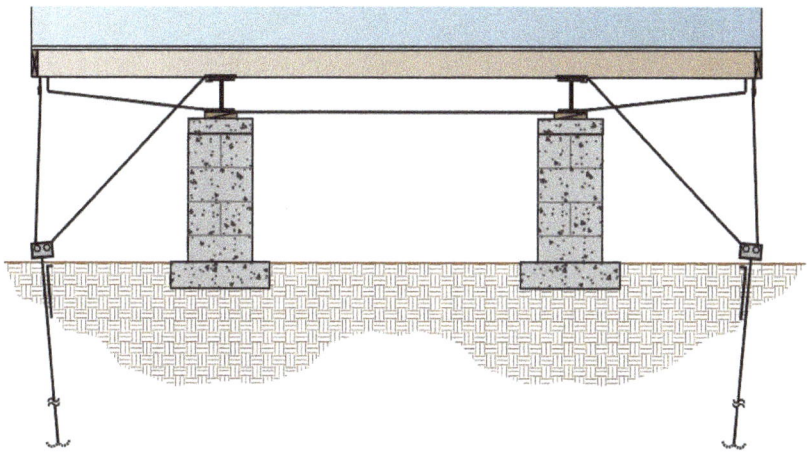

The set-up of a park model must be in compliance with the manufacturer's instructions. But these are usually not available for an inspector, and Florida has a minimum requirement at Administrative Code 15C-1.0102(1): *"The park trailer manufacturer shall make built-in provisions for a minimum of three (3) vertical tie-down straps and three (3) frame tie-down straps on each side of the unit. All used park trailers shall have at least three (3) vertical and three (3) frame tie-down straps installed. Exception: The center vertical tie-down strap on used units may be exempt when it is structurally prohibitive to install."*

Older park models that have been in place for years will not meet this standard. Otherwise, a park model should be evaluated like any mobile home, looking for loose or corroded tie-downs, tears in the belly board, leaning piers, gaps in the skirting, roof leaks, and so forth.

Modular Homes

Modular homes are manufactured in a factory, but are built to local building code standards and installed on a regular foundation. There are two types: on-frame and off-frame. An on-frame is built on steel I-beams similar to a mobile home, while an off-frame is built only on wood framing. The off-frame are installed on a continuous perimeter stem-wall over a footing and center piers, while an on-frame is usually set on piers over a poured footing. All modulars were once off-frame and the on-frame type is a newer design.

But the important thing to know is that both must comply with the building code where they are installed, along with specific standards for modulars. In Florida, it's the Residential Edition of the Florida Building Code (FBC), and then the Department of Community Affairs (DCA) further regulates their construction. There will be a data plate similar to a HUD Data Plate inside the home. Also, in Florida, a DCA Label is affixed inside, like the one shown below. Other states have similar programs.

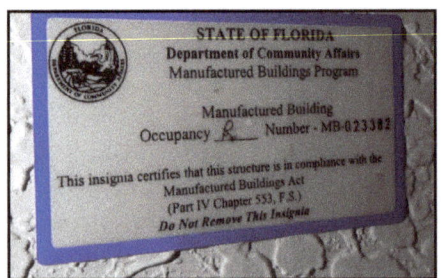

IBTS

The Institute for Building Technology and Safety (IBTS) maintains a data base with all the construction information on manufactured homes built since HUD took over supervision on July 15, 1976. So they are the people to contact if a homebuyer needs to find out or verify any information about a used home, such as:

•• The VIN/serial number, if you give them a HUD tag (Verification Label) number.

•• The HUD tag number(s), if you give them the serial number. But IBTS does not issue replacement HUD tag.

•• A replacement for a missing HUD Performance Certification sheet (data plate), if you provide either the serial number or the HUD tag number(s).

   You can order any of the items from their website at www.ibts.org and, of course, there is a fee—and an additional fee if you want rush service.

Incidentally, the serial number is required by HUD to be stamped into the front cross-beam of the undercarriage of any mobile home built after July 15, 1976, in letters a minimum of 3/8-inches high. But it may be inaccessible or difficult to read due to corrosion.

Second Set Homes

Manufactured homes that have been relocated from the original delivery site from the factory or dealer are called "second set" in the industry. Determining if a home has been moved from its original location is not part of a typical inspection.

But it may be important for the buyer to know whether a resale home has been moved since delivery because FHA, VA, USDA, and many conventional financing providers will not lend on a second set home. If there is any uncertainty, you can give a homebuyer the following instructions to check it.

Go to the Institute for Building Technology and Safety website at ibts.org to find out where the home was originally delivered. Click on "Manufactured Home Certifications" in the menu bar, then "Submit Online Request." It will cost you $50 to get what they call a "Label Verification Letter," which lists the location of the home's first destination from the factory or retail dealer center.

The verification letter also lists label number(s), serial number(s), date of manufacture, and name of manufacturer. Standard processing takes 10 working days (two weeks). But, if you want it faster, it's $100 for three days and $175 for one day delivery. These prices are, of course, subject to change over time. See previous page for more on IBTS offerings.

Pre-Inspection for Moving a Used Home

We lived in a small rural county in North Florida years ago, and their acceptance of just about any ancient single-wide that could be dragged onto a property meant that a rusty hulk could appear next door at any time. People naturally take pride in their manufactured home and want to protect their investment; so making sure that a new neighbor doesn't become the local eyesore is important.

That's why building departments with zoning that allows manufactured homes now require a "pre-inspection" to be done before a used home is allowed to be moved into their area. Here's an example of a two-page pre-inspection form for Sumter County, Florida.

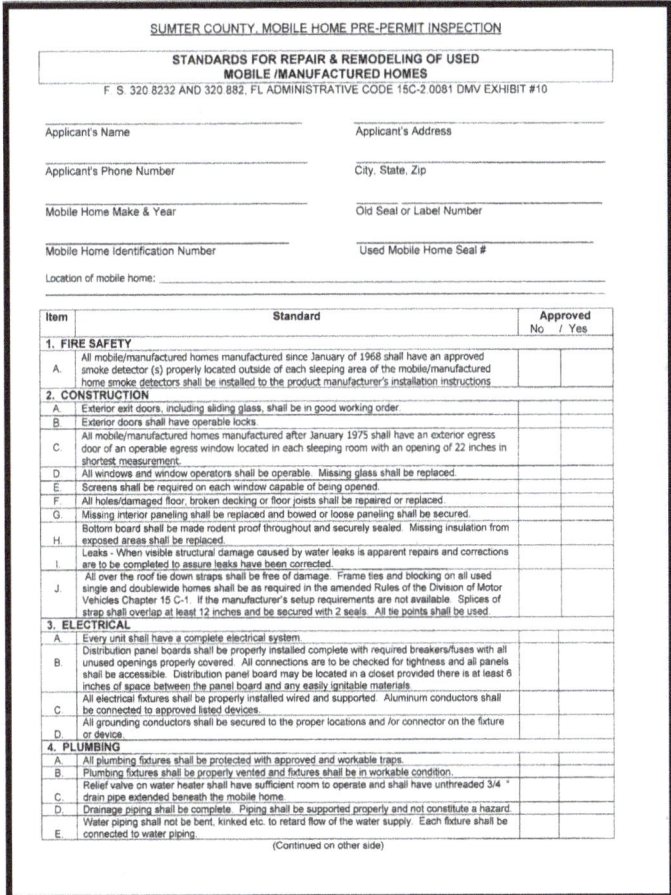

		No	Yes
5. HEATING & AIR CONDITIONING			
A	All required cooking/heating appliances shall be properly anchored and connected in place.		
B	If the home has deleted heating system, drop-outs must be installed for connecting exterior system.		
C	All homes with central heating/cooling shall have operable thermostat.		
D	Air registers shall be operable.		
E	Ducts shall be sealed at openings and shall not be crushed or missing.		
F	Gas furnace/water heating vents shall be properly installed and secured to appliance.		
G	There shall be proper return air to furnace, exterior heat/AC units and all rooms.		
H	Range/bathroom ceiling vents shall be complete and vented to outside.		
I	All gas appliances shall be connected with an approved shut-off valve, if home was manufactured after May of 1975.		

PROVIDE COMMENTS ON ITEMS NOT APPROVED

Item	Comment

All inspections and certifications shall be performed by a mobile home dealer licensed in Florida, engineer, architect, certified or registered, residential, building, or general contractor, or by a building inspector/ Building Official certified by Florida. (MUST SUBMIT COPY OF LICENSE)

The home shall not be moved onto the parcel which permitting is sought prior to this "pre-permit inspection" and permitting.

Homes inspected but not certified shall only be permitted after the permittee agrees, in writing, to correct all items found not in compliance with the above referenced guidelines.

I hereby certify that I have personally inspected the above-described mobile home and that the condition of same is as described herein.

_____ _____/ /_____ _____
Business Name   Inspector Name: Print & Signature   Date

I hereby certify that I have personally inspected the above-described mobile home and that the condition of same meets or exceeds all of the above described standards.

_____ _____/ /_____ _____
Business Name   Certifying Name: Print & Signature   Date

Sumter County Building Department
7375 Powell Road, Suite 115 Wildwood, FL 34785
Phone Number 352-689-4460
Fax Number 352-689-4461

They typically require that the form be filled out by a licensed construction professional or inspector before moving the home or before installation at the site. Any defects found during the inspection need to be repaired before the move is allowed. Some jurisdictions may even have a specific age limit for moving a used home, ranging upward from as low as 5 years, but most don't.

The home is inspected again by the local building inspector after piers, tie-downs, code steps, and utility connections are complete at the new homesite.

This type of inspection can be a profitable sideline, especially if you connect with a local mobile home installer that does a lot of relocations. But be sure you have the type of license required to certify a pre-permit report before accepting the work.

Tie-Down Certifications

Many lenders and insurance companies are now requiring a tie-down certification report before they will mortgage or insure an older manufactured home. It's formally called a "HUD Compliant Foundation Engineering Certification," and its purpose is to verify that an older mobile home meets the requirements for a permanent foundation as defined by the Permanent Foundations Guide for Manufactured Housing HUD Publication dated September 1996.

The certification must be done by an engineer licensed in the state where the manufactured home is located. There are multiple national companies that specialize in tie-down certifications, and they can be easily found with a Google search. Many of them will partner with local home inspectors to do the on-site documentation and photography for a portion of the fee, and this is another opportunity for additional income for inspectors of manufactured homes.

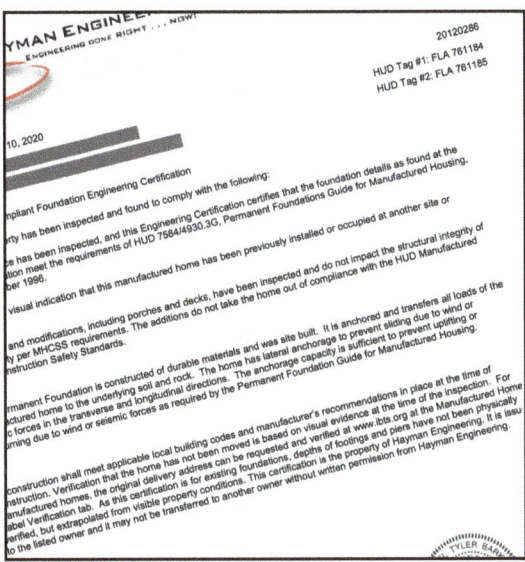

www.ingramcontent.com/pod-product-compliance
Lightning Source LLC
Chambersburg PA
CBHW040222040426
42333CB00050B/3290